Physics Fun
For Younger Ones

by KK Stoltz

Illustrated by A. Shiosaky

By Grace For Glory Publishing, LLC

Pittsburgh, PA

www.bygraceforglorylit.com

ISBN: 9780998730226

Dedicated to:

Mr. Weaver and Mrs. Pugliese,
my high school physics teachers, thank you for
seeing something in me I couldn't see myself.

And my little scientists, you and
the conservation of angular momentum
make my world go round.

Forces

FORCES are everywhere.
They are easily found.
If there's a push or a pull,
then a force is around.

There are so many kinds.
Let's learn a few.
There's gravity, normal,
and contact force too!

GRAVITY is special.
It pulls down from the sky,
and keeps us from flying,
no matter how hard we try.

A NORMAL force happens
when two objects touch.
That are still, not moving,
and resting, as such.

CONTACT forces are common,
not hard to discover.
They happen when one object
pushes or pulls another.

Like shoving a box
across the floor,
or dragging a wagon,
or slamming a door.

All forces are VECTORS,
so along with how strong,
we can know the direction
of a force moving along.

Gravity always points down,
and a normal force points away
from where objects touch
in the spot, where they stay.

Let's learn another word.
I must insist it.
TORQUE measures force
applied at a distance.

The further from a pivot
a force is applied,
you'll be pleased to find out,
the less you have tried!

When closing a door
always push from the end.
It is so much easier
far away from the hinge.

We've learned lots about forces.
We're off to a great start.
Be proud of all you know now.
You're really, very smart!

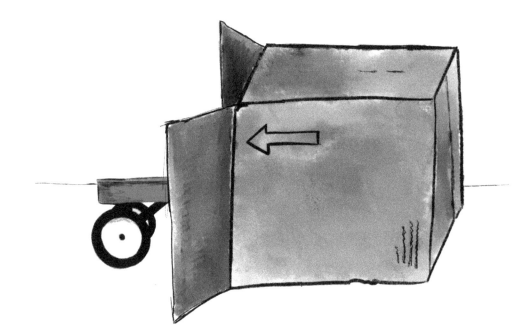

Motion

Every day you see MOTION,
all around, up and down.

Balls bounce, cups fall,
and cars drive through town.

A man named Newton
studied objects in motion.
He gave us three laws
that caused quite a commotion.

Newton's laws don't need
a policeman to obey.
These rules are natural.
Things just happen this way.

The first law is easy!
It makes so much sense.
If an object is resting, so it will sit.
If it moves, it keeps moving.
It won't slow, not one bit.

Until a net force is applied,
Then WAHOO!
Its movement will change.
That's always true!

The object will speed up
or slow down in relation.
We call this change
ACCELERATION!

Law number two is so fun to say.
The net force on an object equals
M – A.

M is for MASS and
A – ACCELERATION.
When Newton found this law
it was time for celebration!

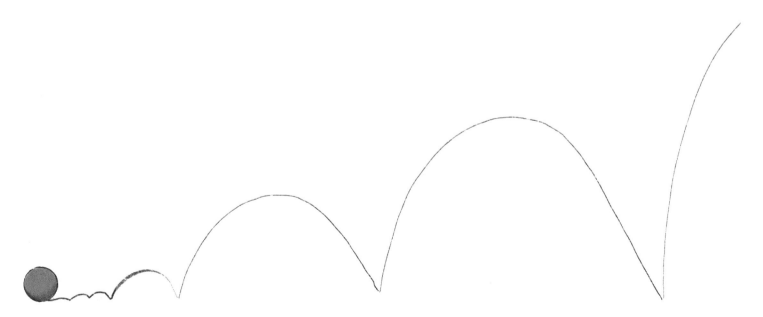

The last of Newton's laws
is important too.
When there's a force
on an object,
there are actually two!

For every single force
to an object applied,
an equal and opposite force
comes from inside.

That's why when you paddle
riding in a canoe,
you push water back
but go forward too.

So, there you have it!
Laws numbered 1, 2, and 3!
How neat is the science
around you and me!

Have you ever heard of ENERGY?
Did you have any clue…
that energy makes everything
work around you?

The food in your belly.
The lights on the wall.
The warmth from your oven.
Energy is a part of it all.

Energy is a word,
and it's used very often.
But sometimes its real meaning
can be forgotten.

In science, it tells us
how much work can be done.
It's measured in Joules
and can be really fun!

Everything you can hold
has mass and energy shared.
They're related by an equation:
$E=mc^2$

Energy has many types,
this much is true.
It can't be created
or destroyed by you.

It won't magically appear.
It never goes away.
It's always CONSERVED
each and every day.

One type of energy
that's good to know
comes from objects in motion,
no matter how slow.

KINETIC energy is its name,
and please do believe,
it depends on an object's mass
and the speed it achieves.

POTENTIAL energy is stored
and depends on position.
It measures what might happen
if we change some conditions.

An apple at the top of a very tall tree
has so much potential. It's full of energy.

If it falls from the branch
and tumbles to the ground,
its potential will be changed
into a crash, thump, splat sound.

THERMAL energy comes
from an object's inside,
as tiny particles wiggle
and start to collide.

Whenever someone pours
hot tea in a cup,
thermal energy warms
the cup's surface right up.

Sometimes the best way
to understand words you hear
is to talk about the places
you'll see them appear.

So, let's talk about fun rides,
and you will see
they have potential, kinetic,
and thermal energy!

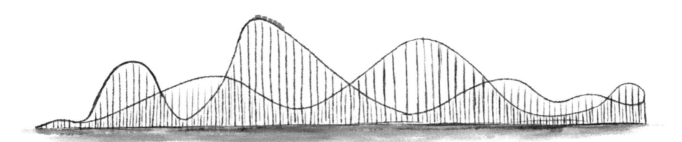

When the ride is up
at the top of its hill,
it's full of potential,
the potential to thrill!

As it starts to move
whooshing down toward the ground,
it's kinetic energy
that can be easily found!

FRICTION does work
as the ride warms its track.
It creates thermal energy
that you will never get back.

Now it's your turn
to find some ways
that energy shows up
in each of your days!

Sound

Stop and listen.
What do you hear?
Sound that is far?
Sound that is near?

SOUND is an amazing,
invisible thing.
It's heard with our ears
when a doorbell rings.

It's made up of energy,
all stored in a WAVE.
You can't see it or taste it
or keep it to save.

Sound waves are special,
the LONGITUDINAL kind.
They move more like a worm
than a snake you might find.

There are 3 fancy words
that can tell us a lot
about all the qualities
that sound waves have got.

AMPLITUDE tells us
about the wave's size.
Small for a whisper.
Big for loud cries.

WAVELENGTH and FREQUENCY
are the other two words.
They determine the pitch
of each sound that is heard.

The PITCH of a sound can be high or low.
Like the high, pretty pitch of a piccolo.

Or the low, deep pitch
of a bass guitar.
Different pitches can be
heard wherever you are.

When a loud thing moves toward you, you won't believe this,
the sound wave itself actually gets squished!

And if that's not enough,
when the noise moves away,
the sound wave is stretched,
like a slinky at play.

This change that we hear
and have come to expect
is something that's known
as the DOPPLER EFFECT.

Now that you've learned
more about sound,
Get up! Go explore!
Listen around!

Make sound of your own
or sound with a toy
and think of all the science
you get to enjoy!

What exactly is LIGHT?
And what does it do?
Well if you are wondering,
this book is for you!

Light comes from the sun,
so shiny and bright.
It helps us see in the day,
but not much at night.

Light can come from a lamp
or a bulb in the ceiling.
When you're warmed on the beach,
that's light that you're feeling.

You can't always see light.
Its spectrum is vast,
with radio waves, x-rays,
then gamma rays come last.

It just so happens
that those are light too.
Even microwave ovens
use light to heat food.

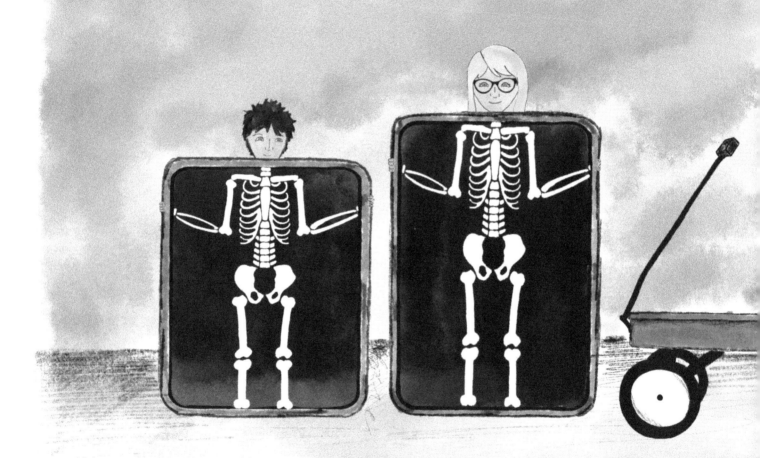

The radio in your car,
a remote for TV,
a call on your phone
all use light you can't see.

The light that we're used to,
the light that we know,
is called visible light
and makes everything glow.

Light is mysterious,
but it's very important.
It supplies us with energy.
There's many uses for it.

Plants turn light into food,
so they can grow tall.
That's called PHOTOSYNTHESIS.
Light powers it all.

When light shines through raindrops
floating up high,
a beautiful rainbow
appears in the sky.

A rainbow is light
that REFLECTS and REFRACTS,
which really just means
it was bent and bounced back.

Light can act like a particle
and sometimes a wave.
Even scientists get confused
by the way light behaves.

So the next time you flip
a light switch or two,
remember all the cool things
you've learned light can do!

The End.

CPSIA information can be obtained
at www.ICGtesting.com
Printed in the USA
LVHW072306290419
616027LV00011B/578/P

9 780998 730226